Dr. Carl Menger

Foundations of Economic Science:
The Ultimate Guide to Understanding
Capital

C&P Books

# Inhaltsverzeichnis

*Preface by Dr. Vladek Beksiński* ............................... 1

*Introduction* ............................................................. 6

*I: The main criteria for the classification of economic sciences* ...................................................... 11

*II: The historical economic sciences must be separated in presentation from the theoretical, morphological, and practical ones* ......................... 17

*III: The idea of uniting theoretical and practical economic sciences in a systematic presentation* .... 19

*IV: Are independent morphological sciences justified in the field of economic phenomena?* ........ 24

*V: Overview of the System of Economic sciences* .. 30

*VI: The Systematics of Economic Sciences under the Methodological Perspective of the Historical School* ......................................................................... 32

*VII: The Systematics of Economic Sciences from the Methodological Perspective of the Historical School (Continuation)* ......................................................... 41

*VIII: In defense against some recent attacks directed at my methodological standpoint* ............ 47

# Preface by Dr. Vladek Beksiński

In an era marked by rapid change and unprecedented complexity, where the delicate interplay between theory and practice often resembles a chaotic ballet, the exploration of economic thought becomes not just a scholarly pursuit but an audacious act of intellectual rebellion. As we find ourselves at the crossroads of tradition and innovation, it is both necessary and audacious to delve deep into the foundations of economic inquiry with a discerning eye, challenging the status quo that has too long reigned unchallenged in the realm of economic sciences.

This work dared to confront the existing paradigms, shaking the very roots of accepted methodologies and calling into question the foundations upon which they stand. It is particularly fitting that we reflect on the legacy of Dr. Carl Menger, whose groundbreaking ideas revolutionized our understanding of economics and laid the groundwork for the Austrian School of economic thought. Menger's emphasis on the subjective nature of value and the importance of individual choices continues to resonate deeply, challenging us to reconsider how we analyze economic phenomena in light of human behavior and social dynamics.

Herein lies a clarion call for intellectual rigor, a manifesto for the bold thinkers and the inquisitive minds who believe that economic theory should not merely exist in the sterile confines of academia but should pulse with the vitality and urgency of real-world application. In a world that is constantly evolving, it is our responsibility as scholars and practitioners to ensure that our approaches remain equally dynamic and responsive.

As we navigate the labyrinthine complexities of social phenomena, we must confront the disheartening reality that theoretical frameworks have often been relegated to the sidelines, overshadowed by their practical counterparts. This relegation has fostered a disconnect between the insights of economic theory and the pressing needs of society. Yet, it is precisely in this interplay that the true essence of economic inquiry resides. We stand at a pivotal moment, where the profound need for a robust methodology in social sciences beckons us to engage deeply, provocatively, and creatively with our subject matter.

This preface serves not merely as an introduction; it is a proclamation of intellectual intent. The time for complacency is over. The intricate tapestry of economic life cannot be adequately addressed by those who choose to observe from a distance, content with mere descriptions of past institutions and efforts. Instead, we must embrace the challenge of shaping a future informed by both rigorous theoretical insight and the ingenuity of practical application.

In these pages, you will encounter a spirited defense of the economic sciences, an impassioned argument for the necessity of marrying abstract thought with tangible realities. Here, we unveil the shortcomings of previous methodologies while advocating for an expansive, dynamic approach to economic theory—one that is not only rooted in historical context but is also daringly forward-looking. This is an invitation to reimagine how we understand economic phenomena and to challenge the limitations of conventional wisdom.

As we reflect on Menger's contributions, we are reminded that the evolution of economic thought is not merely an academic exercise; it is a vital endeavor that influences policies and practices shaping our societies. Prepare to embark on a transformative journey that intertwines intellectual bravado with a steadfast commitment to understanding the complexities of human economic behavior. This is not just another treatise; it is a bold step towards redefining what it means to master the art of economics in a world that demands more than mere survival—it demands innovation, resilience, and above all, a willingness to confront uncomfortable truths.

As we peel back the layers of established thought, we will challenge the assumptions that have long gone unexamined. We will delve into the intricate relationships between various economic actors, scrutinizing the interplay of policies, practices, and theories that shape our collective economic reality. We will explore how theoretical frameworks can not only inform but also empower those on the frontlines of economic decision-making, enabling them to craft solutions that resonate with the needs of their communities.

This exploration will be marked by a robust dialogue between theory and practice, highlighting the indispensable role that each plays in shaping a comprehensive understanding of economics. We will not shy away from the complexities and contradictions inherent in this field; rather, we will embrace them, recognizing that they are essential to the richness of economic discourse. Our inquiry will reveal the multifaceted nature of economic phenomena, illuminating the pathways through which we can arrive at actionable insights that are not only theoretically sound but also practically viable.

As we embark on this journey together, I invite you to engage with the ideas presented herein with an open mind and a critical eye. Allow yourself to question, to challenge, and to envision new possibilities. This is not just a scholarly pursuit; it is a call to action for anyone who believes in the power of economics to effect meaningful change in our world.

Welcome to the frontier of economic thought. Buckle up; it's going to be an exhilarating ride. Here, we will not only dissect the complexities of economic theory but also pave the way for a transformative understanding of the role that economics plays in our lives. This is the beginning of a new chapter in the exploration of economic sciences—one that promises to be as provocative as it is enlightening: The enduring legacy of Dr. Carl Menger.

# Introduction

The discussion about the epistemology and methods of economics has not settled since the publication of my "Investigations into the Method of the Social Sciences." In numerous writings, lectures, and public presentations, my methodological stance has been met with repeated opposition and critical reviews. My specific arguments about the system of tasks that social research must address in the field of economics, and the closely related issue of classifying economic sciences, have also received friendly approval, even though much opposition still exists. Even the sharp misunderstandings, which one might expect to provoke questions of a general nature, would not persuade me to remain silent in this debate. On the contrary, given the current state of national economic studies in Germany, I am firmly convinced that we will only achieve full clarity on the entire system of tasks that economic science must address if we maintain our focus on unity and avoid the disastrous consequences of abandoning such unity for both practical life and pure scientific inquiry.

The historical school describes the origin and historical course of social phenomena and — apart from a few particularly biased authors — strives earnestly to arrive at the laws of these phenomena in the sense of external regularities in the coexistence and sequence of social phenomena.

They are thus focused on analyzing the complex economic phenomena by tracing them back to their final psychological and political factors, without neglecting to explain to us the theoretical understanding of those phenomena. In many instances, however, their attempt to derive knowledge of the actual economic phenomena from the complex coexistence of psychological constructs falls short, because they fail to consider the fact that economic phenomena must be analyzed based on their own specific laws. Many instances of misinterpretation, as well as the effort to reach an understanding of real economic phenomena solely by linking them to psychological constructs, result from this approach. The historical school's reluctance to apply theoretical analysis has led to a blurring of the lines between theoretical and empirical work.

The disregard of theoretical economic work has caused a large disadvantage for national-economic research, preventing it from dealing with the broader and more concrete economic processes of the modern era. It must be noted that the historical method cannot replace theoretical investigation, and the fact that the development of economic phenomena follows certain laws should not be overlooked. The historical school has not succeeded in finding theoretical approaches to economic analysis, but only in applying descriptive methods. While the historical method has its place in understanding social processes, the failure to consider theoretical analysis, especially of social phenomena, has weakened the potential insights that economic research could provide.

The misunderstanding of the nature of economic phenomena and the neglect of a theoretical approach have thus delayed the ability to address crucial political and economic problems effectively. Solving these methodological issues is an urgent need for the discipline.

However, I will not discuss the theory of economic phenomena and the pressing tasks related to it at this point, despite the attacks I have recently encountered. Instead, I will respond by focusing on another issue. The investigation of the nature of theoretical economics, its various branches, and the specific tasks conditioned by the nature of economic phenomena seems to me a task that, in light of the current state of methodological research, is both urgent and enticing to address. Any attempt to tackle this problem, however, is doomed to fail as long as the question of the position of economic theory within the broader framework of economics remains unresolved. The historical school has not yet adequately addressed the specific tasks posed by the interplay of history and statistics, on one hand, and the theoretical and practical tasks of economics, on the other.

The essential unity of the major branches of economic research—history, theory, and practice—has not been sufficiently recognized. By failing to strictly separate the "method of historical investigation" from the so-called "historical method in theoretical and practical economics," the distinct nature of economic science in terms of its tasks has not been properly understood. The historical school has not provided a clear distinction between economic theory and the organization of empirical and statistical research, which remains an urgent need for further scientific exploration.

It has neither strictly distinguished between the "method of historical research" and the so-called "historical method in theoretical and practical economic sciences" nor correctly recognized the unique position of practical economic sciences within the system of tasks that our science must solve. An organized aggregation of historical, statistical, theoretical, morphological, and practical elements, concerning economic knowledge, seems to be considered the only worthwhile goal of scientific presentation. Who would want to deal with this system of tasks, specifically the theoretical economic sciences, before clarifying the position of the latter within the broader framework of economic sciences—before the classification of economic sciences is fundamentally clarified?

# I: The main criteria for the classification of economic sciences

The division of the results of realist research into individual sciences has generally occurred in two fundamentally different directions: on the one hand, according to the nature of the objects of research, depending on the various domains of the real world on which scientific inquiry focuses, and on the other hand, according to the different directions of scientific inquiry, based on the varying perspectives of the real world.

The division of sciences into natural and human sciences, the subdivision of natural sciences into those dealing with organic and inorganic nature, and further into those dealing with the different areas of the organic and inorganic world (petrography, botany, zoology, etc.), as well as the emergence of distinct fields like law, state, society, and economics, are based on the first classification principle.

However, the progress of the sciences and the deeper engagement with the diverse problems of realist inquiry has led to a further subdivision of the sciences, which follows the second classification principle. In each area of the real world, different directions of inquiry have emerged, which, as they have matured, have developed into distinct branches of research and, depending on the needs for specialized presentation of their results, have led to the creation of distinct sciences.

The quest for understanding the real world manifests itself in two fundamental directions with regard to each domain of phenomena.

It can be directed:

1. towards the understanding of concrete phenomena and their specific relationships in space and time, and
2. towards the understanding of the general nature of phenomena and their general interrelationships (the coexistence and succession of generally determined phenomena).

The first direction of research leads, depending on whether the concrete phenomena in the various fields of the real world are considered from the perspective of their static state or their development, to the statistical or historical sciences. The second, depending on whether the general nature of the phenomena (the common characteristics of the phenomena!) or the relationships and inner connections of generally determined phenomena (the laws of phenomena) are the subject of our scientific inquiry, leads to the morphological or theoretical sciences.

However, our scientific interest is not confined to merely understanding and comprehending the real world. Alongside the aforementioned directions of research, in every field of the real world, there is also a pursuit of establishing the principles and methods for appropriately shaping phenomena (for purposeful intervention in the course of things), the systematically ordered results of which we refer to as the practical or applied sciences.

These different approaches to knowledge—statistical, historical, morphological, theoretical, and practical—are not peculiar to various domains of the real world but are distinct to each individual domain. Accordingly, the sciences are differentiated by the various formal natures of their truths, within these main categories, and further subdivided into specialized disciplines.

The classification of the natural sciences based on the different fields of natural objects, on the one hand, and the various directions of inquiry, on the other, has been partly completed for some time and is still developing. No one confuses, in the realm of natural research, the description of concrete natural objects in their static state or the course of historically significant natural events with a morphology of natural phenomena, even if the subject matter pertains to the same field of phenomena—for example, the history of the animal kingdom with systematic zoology or anthropohistory with the morphology of human races.

Likewise, natural science distinguishes the morphological from the theoretical natural sciences, such as systematic petrography, botany, zoology, and anatomy from physics, chemistry, and physiology. The same applies to the distinction between theoretical and practical sciences. A natural scientist does not confuse chemistry with chemical engineering, mechanics and physics with so-called mechanical technology, or anatomy and physiology with surgery and therapy.

Practical considerations in organizing scientific material or the underdeveloped state of a particular branch of research may, in some cases, lead to the combination of results from different approaches in scientific presentations, even in the realm of natural sciences. However, no natural scientist would ever think of progressing towards a single, unified natural science that encompasses all statistical-historical, morphological, theoretical, and practical knowledge as a naturally ordered aggregate of all knowledge related to nature or even to a specific field of it.

The difference between historical-statistical, morphological, theoretical, and practical sciences—further subdivided within these main categories—is beyond question for any thinking natural scientist. Similarly, in the field of political science, for example, there is no doubt about the difference between statistics, the history of states, political theory, and politics, just as in the field of law there is no question about the distinction between legal history, legal dogmatics, and legislative policy.

In the field of economics, the above-mentioned development is still incomplete in many respects and is only in the process of becoming. The division of economics into historical-statistical, morphological, theoretical, and applied sciences has not yet become a common practice in presentations. Indeed, the mixing of historical-statistical descriptions, morphological representations, "laws of economic phenomena," and principles and methods for purposeful action in economics still remains the norm in economic literature, while the separation of economic sciences according to the formal nature of their truths is rather the exception. Moreover, this practice is not only due to considerations of practicality—such as for didactic reasons or in writings aimed at popular instruction—but, as must be emphasized, it is also maintained in works that claim to present themselves as strictly scientific.

The explanation for this fact lies primarily in the underdeveloped state of economic sciences so far. Many other disciplines also exhibited a similar phenomenon in their earlier developmental phases, presenting aggregates of knowledge from historical-statistical, morphological, theoretical, and practical approaches, arranged by external factors and pertaining to a specific field of phenomena. In other areas of research, the disciplines corresponding to different formal approaches to knowledge only gradually and through fluctuating attempts separated and developed into independent sciences.

The natural course of the development of scientific knowledge will inevitably lead, as in all other areas of research, to a division of economics along the lines previously outlined, as soon as the importance of systematics for presentation and especially for understanding the inner connections of the results of scientific research is recognized by economic writers. Furthermore, the impossibility of systematically presenting results from different approaches (in a single system!) will become clear to those working in our field.

## II: The historical economic sciences must be separated in presentation from the theoretical, morphological, and practical ones

What has hindered the above development in German economics, and in fact pushed back some of the progress already made, is the inadequate methodological understanding of the historical school in many respects. Our historical economists envision the idea of a **universal science of economics** that encompasses all knowledge related to economics in a single, unified presentation. They do not accept any separation in presentation, which would in no way disrupt the internal connections of these sciences. On the contrary, they often regard such separation as a regression, calling it an "unnatural division of inherently connected material," or they interpret any principle of dividing economic sciences in such a way that it is essentially negated.

Such a universal science of economics is not only an absurdity from the standpoint of scientific systematics, but if the above demand for such a presentation is taken seriously, it becomes downright impossible. I will not go into the notion of treating economic history and economic statistics within a system of political economy that also includes the morphological, theoretical, and practical knowledge related to economics; that idea is utterly fanciful. I would be curious to see a system of political economy—or even a reasonably ordered presentation of this science—that also encompasses the entire scope of economic history and economic statistics of all times and all nations. The independent presentation of economic history and economic policy is an absolute necessity. And this is the issue here—not the mere use of historical-statistical facts to exemplify theoretical and practical truths of political economy, or the use of history and statistics as foundational auxiliary sciences to political economy.

Even those concise presentations of economic history and the literature of political economy, which are often placed at the beginning of our scientific works, do not contradict the above viewpoint. They are merely introductions to the study of political economy—overviews of the relevant fields of knowledge intended to serve the above didactic purpose—which in no way negate the necessity of an independent presentation of economic history, economic statistics, and the history of economic literature, nor can they somehow replace such independent presentations. It is a misunderstanding to claim that the history and statistics of economics, as independent sciences, could be treated within a system of "Political Economy" that encompasses morphology, theory, and practical economic sciences.

## III: The idea of uniting theoretical and practical economic sciences in a systematic presentation

Even the idea of uniting theoretical economics and economic policy into a systematically presented science, upon closer consideration, raises serious concerns. Each of these two disciplines has its own system, corresponding to the different formal nature of their truths. Combining the two in one presentation forces either the ordering of the truths of economic policy according to the system of theoretical economics—treating the principles and procedures of economic policy related to specific economic phenomena (closely tied to theoretical knowledge!) as part of the presentation of economic laws—or conversely, accompanying the systematic presentation of economic policy with occasional theoretical explanations. Both approaches are not only possible but, as extensive experience shows, also practically feasible. However, anyone who considers the history of the development of scientific knowledge and understands the importance of separating scientific knowledge based on its formal nature for the methodology and systematization of the sciences will recognize this as merely a symptom of the still undeveloped state of economics.

What I accuse my opponents of is their misunderstanding of this fact. Their error lies in portraying the merging of theoretical and practical economic sciences as a progress, as a methodological demand for our science, while all of us should be striving to promote the separation of theoretical and practical knowledge in scientific presentation, which is so crucial for the development of the latter, wherever it is not yet advisable, due to the underdeveloped state of our science, to at least prepare for it. However, some of our historical economists depict this development as a regression and present this reversal as an achievement of science.

What Fr. J. Neumann argues for the opposite standpoint is untenable. It is incorrect to claim that the separation of economics into theoretical and practical parts would "lead to unnecessary repetitions." This opinion is based on the widely held prejudice among German economists that every single science must offer all the research results relating to a particular field of phenomena, rather than recognizing that there are sciences which already assume knowledge of other sciences. Physiology assumes knowledge of anatomy; surgery and therapy assume knowledge of both of these first-named sciences; chemical technology assumes knowledge of chemistry; mechanics requires knowledge of mathematics, and so on. The belief that the division of sciences based on their formal nature would lead to repetitions is so mistaken that the exact opposite is true. Once the practitioners of our science understand that it is not a haphazard and arbitrary aggregation of theoretical and practical knowledge, arranged by external factors, but rather a presentation of the results of scientific research related to economics in a complete and systematically ordered manner, reflecting their internal coherence, the separation of theoretical and practical sciences will prove to be the shortest path to achieving the aforementioned goal.

Even less can the circumstance highlighted by Neumann, that separating our science into a theoretical and a practical part would often require distinct definitions for each part, be considered a valid objection against this separation. If this is indeed the case, then establishing these "concepts" in question as distinct is precisely a task for our science, one that must be solved, and avoiding this task certainly cannot be considered a scientific solution. Neumann does not seem fully aware of the sensitive issue he has touched upon in our science. It is true that the most important economic concepts are applied in significantly different ways in theoretical and practical economic sciences. Just think of the concepts of capital, interest on capital, land rent, and so on, and how they are applied in theory on one hand, and in public finance and tax theory (particularly in the theory of income taxes) on the other. But is this confusion really an argument against separating economic theory from practical economics?

If Neumann finally wants to apply the same principle of separating economics into theoretical and practical parts to divide "Political Economy" into a general and a specialized part, this too, as I have already demonstrated elsewhere, is based on a methodological misunderstanding. Both theoretical and practical economics each have a general and a specialized part. Just as chemical technology cannot be considered a special part of chemistry, nor surgery a special part of anatomy, practical economics cannot be regarded as a special part of theoretical economics, and vice versa, theoretical economics cannot be seen as the general part of practical economics.

It is true that even when theoretical and practical economic teachings are treated together—however imperfect that system may be—a general and a special part must emerge, as is the case with any organized presentation of a science. However, this fact does not affect the decision on our question in any way. The separation of political economy, or any specific branch of economics, into a general and a special part, and the separation of economics into theoretical and practical sciences, are two entirely distinct methodological problems.

The former pertains to the internal systematics of each economic science, while the latter refers to the classification of economics as a whole.

## IV: Are independent morphological sciences justified in the field of economic phenomena?

It seems less certain to me whether the development of economic sciences will lead to an independent, systematic morphology of economic phenomena, and what role the results of the morphological approach to research will play in the overall system of economic sciences.

Not all theoretical disciplines correspond to independent morphological sciences. Even in natural sciences, some theoretical natural sciences—those that are essentially the result of the analytical-synthetic method (such as chemistry and physics)—have no distinct morphological counterparts. Rightly, W. Wundt points out, regarding the question of the actual separation of individual branches in the system of natural sciences, that, for example, the classification of chemical compounds is not usually separated from the theory of chemical phenomena.

However, when Wundt explains this "peculiar circumstance" by referring on the one hand to the relatively underdeveloped state of chemical science, in which the tasks of description and explanation are not yet sufficiently distinguished, and on the other hand to the entrenched traditions of natural history, where only naturally occurring objects, not artificially created ones, are treated as subjects of distinct systematic sciences, it seems to me that the distinguished epistemologist is overlooking the true cause of this practice, which is also significant for research in the field of economic phenomena.

Morphological knowledge, insofar as it is the result of a real analysis of complex phenomena down to their elementary factors and the isolating synthesis of the latter, has no independent significance. It serves the purpose of theory and is therefore appropriately combined in presentations with the knowledge that brings us to an awareness of the laws governing the synthesis of the respective phenomena (i.e., with the corresponding theoretical sciences). Indeed, the laws in question could not be presented at all without the aforementioned morphological knowledge. The combination of the results of both directions of research in systematic presentation is thus not only a demand of practicality but also a consequence of their internal coherence.

It is different in cases where the task is not to understand complex natural phenomena through analysis and isolating synthesis, but, at least initially and directly, to describe them, such as in the fields of geology, botany, zoology, etc. Here, the description of forms of appearance—the morphology of the respective fields—gains independent significance, and the consolidation of research results into distinct systematic sciences reflects the independent interest we take in the above-mentioned knowledge.

A similar problem also presents itself in the field of economic phenomena. Here, too, the question is not whether the morphological approach to research is justified—there is no doubt about that—but whether a morphology of economic phenomena has an independent interest alongside economic theory and whether the former should be assigned an independent position alongside the latter in the system of economic sciences.

The answer to this question arises, in agreement with the actual development of economic research so far, from the methodological principles described above. The elementary factors of economic phenomena, which we arrive at through theoretical analysis of complex economic phenomena, have no independent significance in the system of scientific results of economic research. A morphology of these factors does not correspond to any independent scientific need.

Rightly, they are combined in presentations with theoretical economics, insofar as the latter teaches us the laws governing the synthesis of elementary economic phenomena. What is often presented under the title of "fundamental concepts of economics" at the beginning of systematic presentations of theoretical economics, and which is incorporated by the stricter systematizers of our science into their frameworks, is essentially nothing more than an exposition of the nature of the elementary factors of complex economic phenomena. An independent morphology of these factors is no more necessary or useful in scientific terms than it would be in the case of elementary natural phenomena and the compounds formed through isolating synthesis.

However, in cases where the objective is not so much to understand complex economic phenomena through analytic-synthetic research, but rather to describe these phenomena in all their complexity, including the influences of non-economic factors, a systematic morphology of such phenomena indeed seems to possess an independent scientific interest. Alongside the pursuit of theoretical understanding of economic phenomena, and even long before this need is fully recognized in research, there exists a desire to understand these phenomena in their real-world complexity as presented to us through experience, as well as in the variety resulting from various geographical and temporal influences. In this context, morphology supplements the system of economic sciences. It aims to provide a systematic overview of complex economic phenomena where historical sciences can only offer a collective picture of specific economic phenomena within certain spatial boundaries.

Although the efforts to establish a morphology of economic phenomena are still quite modest, and although it is beyond doubt that the results of this research direction can and indeed should be integrated into the more specialized parts of economic theory, especially given the current state of the discipline, the idea does not seem hopeless to me. Morphological studies in the field of economic phenomena may rise above their current stage of dependency or monographic treatment and eventually develop into an independent, systematic economic science of their own.

This is because the complexity of economic phenomena demands not only theoretical insights into their underlying laws but also a clear, organized approach to understanding the multifaceted nature of these phenomena. Whether influenced by geographical, historical, or social factors, the diverse forms in which economic phenomena present themselves to us cannot be fully captured by theory alone. Hence, a systematic economic morphology could help fill this gap by providing a structured, comprehensive view of the various ways economic processes manifest in reality.

Thus, while the current state of the field may not yet fully accommodate such a morphology, its potential future role within the broader framework of economic sciences remains promising. Through further development, these morphological studies could stand alongside theoretical and practical economics, contributing to a more complete understanding of economic phenomena and their variations across different contexts and periods.

# V: Overview of the System of Economic sciences

A complete system of realistic economic sciences thus includes:

**The historical sciences of economics:**

Economic statistics and economic history, where the former investigates concrete economic phenomena within specific geographical boundaries from the perspective of their current state, and the latter from the perspective of their development, aiming to consolidate these into a unified (collective) picture.

**The morphology of economic phenomena:**

This discipline's task is the classification of real economic phenomena (by types, categories, and subcategories) and the representation of their general nature (the description of common characteristics of various groups of similar phenomena).

**The theory of economic phenomena:**

This discipline is responsible for investigating and presenting the laws of economic phenomena (the regularities in the coexistence and succession of economic phenomena and their internal causation). I have emphasized (p. 475 ff.) that the morphology of fundamental economic phenomena is appropriately combined with theory.

**Practical or applied economic sciences:**

These disciplines teach us the principles and methods for the most efficient realization of generally determined economic objectives (considering the diversity of conditions) based on existing scientific insights.

# VI: The Systematics of Economic Sciences under the Methodological Perspective of the Historical School

The systematics of economic sciences are presented quite differently in the methodology of our historical economists. Here, we first encounter the confusion between historiography and sociology, particularly the confusion between economic history and economics (as a branch of sociology). I have already pointed out the different tasks these sciences are meant to address and the impossibility of treating history and statistics—the history of all times and peoples—within a system of sociology, and likewise economic history and economic statistics within a system of economics.

Nevertheless, some social philosophers continue to cling to this error because they view the task of historiography as establishing the laws of development of concrete nations and their cultures, rather than exploring and presenting their actual development. However, this view has long been rejected as an error, as a misunderstanding of the true task of historiography, by the most prominent historians. Roscher's definition of political economy as the "philosophy of economic history" is a belated echo of this outdated historical perspective.

However, the confusion surrounding the relationship between theoretical and practical economic sciences is even greater. Every positivism, even a less one-sided form than that of our historical economists, struggles to find its proper place regarding the practical sciences.

In the classification of the sciences as conceived by A. Comte, one will search in vain for a clear and consistently upheld position on the above question, and the methodology of the historical school also fails to provide a serious solution to the problem. What is the position of administrative science in relation to sociology within the system of social sciences? And what position does the science of economic policy hold in particular, in relation to economic theory within the system of economic sciences? These are questions that the methodology of our discipline cannot dismiss, yet neither the positivism of Comte nor the historicism of German economics has provided a satisfactory answer. The latter has even outright denied the independent significance of practical economic sciences.

It is true that the sciences that teach us the principles and methods for achieving generally determined human objectives do not hold absolute significance in the sense that our historical economists criticize. However, this is not a serious objection against the validity of these disciplines. It is a blatant error to assume that the same methods will lead to the same results under different circumstances, especially in different times and among different peoples, and therefore that these methods hold absolute significance in that sense. Nevertheless, this mistaken view of the nature and tasks of practical sciences does not undermine their legitimacy. Practical sciences are meant to teach us how certain generally determined objectives can be achieved under various typical conditions—under different circumstances, through different methods.

Whether the physiocratic or even the classical school of economics was as deeply entrenched in this error as our historical economists claim, I will leave open for discussion. Others will clarify this point and correct the one-sided treatment of the history of our discipline's doctrines by the historical school with regard to practical teachings, just as has already been done in relation to the history of certain key teachings of economic theory. In any case, the above interpretation of practical economics is an error, an error that in no way challenges the legitimacy of independent practical economic sciences, as defined above.

However: 'The practical sciences—no matter how much they may research and present various methods calculated for different typical purposes and conditions—nevertheless suffer from the shortcoming that they do not account for the uniqueness of concrete cases in which practitioners are called upon to act. In this respect, they suffer from a flawed absolutism of solutions.' This common objection is based on a prejudice, on the mistaken assumption that practical economic sciences, if they exist at all, can only be understood as 'collections of recipes' for concrete cases in which practitioners are required to act.

Practical sciences do not provide 'recipes' for dealing with each individual concrete case. There are no sciences of this type, no sciences that exhaustively encompass the entire richness and complexity of life and its tasks, that prescribe in advance the method for every single concrete case. No practical science—no matter how complete its systematization—can offer such a thing. Such practical sciences, in this sense, are nothing more than a figment of the imagination of our historical economists. What practical sciences teach, and are capable of teaching, are not 'recipes' for concrete cases. Surgery, therapy, technology, and economic policy are not collections of recipes. They teach us how certain generally determined human purposes can be most effectively realized according to the diversity of conditions—how, naturally, different purposes are achieved under similar conditions and similar purposes under different conditions by different methods. However, they do not provide a specific 'recipe' for the concrete case.

The purposes that people pursue have their individual peculiarities in each concrete case; no less so do the circumstances under which these purposes must be realized in a specific situation. These particularities of individual cases in which practitioners are called to act cannot be fully encompassed by any practical science, no matter how specialized its systematization might be.

In these respects, the practitioner is compelled to rely on their insight into the nature and relationships of phenomena, as well as their own inventiveness. Just as practical sciences are generally built upon theory, the scientifically trained practitioner uses their theoretical understanding as a foundation to modify and perfect the methods suggested by practical sciences for generally determined purposes and circumstances, adapting them to the specific requirements of the concrete case. Their knowledge of practical sciences, combined with their theoretical insight, enables them to determine the appropriate course of action for each concrete case—what one might call the "recipe" for the specific situation.

Indeed, practical life, with its ever-changing scenarios and urgencies, often presents cases where practical sciences, in their current state, fail to provide adequate guidance. In such instances, the practitioner must rely solely on their theoretical insight and their own creative problem-solving. There are situations where theoretical understanding of the nature and relationships of things, even in highly developed disciplines like surgery, therapy, or technology, is the practitioner's only support. While developed practical sciences are certainly not mere collections of recipes, when combined with theoretical knowledge, they serve as a guiding star for the scientifically educated practitioner in the countless situations that form the fabric of practical life.

"But then, why do we need practical sciences at all? Aren't they just an unnecessary detour? Wouldn't the practitioner act more efficiently by focusing exclusively on theory, or even just on history, and directly determining the appropriate course of action in each concrete case?"—Whoever thinks this way (and it seems that a similar view has taken root in the minds of our historical economists) misunderstands the demands of practical life. No matter how extensive one's knowledge of history or how deep one's theoretical understanding of the nature and relationships of things, these alone do not equip the practitioner to determine the most effective course of action in each concrete case with the necessary certainty, speed, and completeness. In addition to theoretical insight, one must possess a combinatorial talent and inventiveness, which are rare and only found in a few exceptionally gifted individuals.

The practical sciences provide us with the sum of results derived from the efforts of the most outstanding practical talents—the true practitioners as well as the scholars of practical sciences—focused on determining the appropriate methods for pursuing human goals, as well as the specific experiences gathered in practice. Even where practical sciences, due to their development or new conditions and emerging needs in practical life, and the specific circumstances, do not provide the practitioner with a direct and fundamental guideline for action in a concrete case, they still offer a systematic overview of all methods suitable for achieving similar goals. This makes it easier for the practitioner to choose the means appropriate to their purposes in the given case, based on their theoretical insight.

Thus, practical sciences have a high independent significance alongside theoretical sciences. To question the usefulness of disciplines such as surgery, therapy, technology, or economic policy would demonstrate complete ignorance of the requirements of practical life. These disciplines, which demand the highest degree of sharpness, experience, inventiveness, and dedication from their scholars, should not be dismissed as mere "cookbooks for practical use," as Kleinwächter suggests—a misguided view akin to that of certain practitioners who see theory as nothing more than an empty game of concepts.

*"However, practical sciences are not sciences in the strict sense of the word, but merely scientific studies."*

I believe this objection is merely playing with the word "science." It is true that certain epistemologists have denied these disciplines the status of sciences, on the grounds that only those disciplines that open up our understanding of things and are capable of systematic presentation deserve the name "science"—in the strictest sense of the word. From this standpoint, even history has been denied the status of a science, which is a grave injustice! Particularly regarding practical sciences, this is incorrect because these disciplines, which are indeed suitable for systematic presentation, not only describe the methods for achieving generally determined human purposes but also provide us with an understanding of them.

Practical sciences do not merely enable us to act mechanically; they also make us aware of the reasons behind our actions. By presenting the system of purposes within a particular area of human activity and the methods for achieving them in their internal coherence, these disciplines elevate themselves to the status of sciences in the true sense of the word.

Even if one chooses to deny them the label of "science" in some specific interpretation of the term or refer to them as "mere scientific studies," their independent significance and importance within the realm of scientific knowledge—what truly matters here—remain unaffected by this terminological debate.

## VII: The Systematics of Economic Sciences from the Methodological Perspective of the Historical School (Continuation)

If it is incorrect to claim that practical sciences (in general) and practical economic sciences (in particular) establish general principles "without regard to the uniqueness of circumstances," if it is incorrect to say they are "merely collections of recipes," and if it is incorrect to suggest that they can be replaced by theory or even mere historical studies—when it is firmly established that these sciences hold significant independent importance for our pursuit of knowledge and practical human life, and that their advancement and deepening require as much research talent and diligence as historical, morphological, and theoretical disciplines—what is the reason that these sciences are so vehemently criticized by our historical economists?

They argue that science should concern itself not with what ought to be, but only with what is. Science should teach us what was, what is, and how it came to be, not what it should be. Therefore, disciplines such as surgery, therapy, technology, and economic policy are not considered sciences, and the pursuit of their exploration and perfection is seen as a delusion—because they do not teach us what was, what is, and how it came to be, but rather, based on the understanding of what was and what is, they concern themselves, in a certain sense, with what ought to be.

I hold great respect for positivism in science! It has significantly contributed to liberating us from aprioristic speculation in the sciences aimed at understanding the real world. However, I would not see the fact that positivism stands in a critical light toward practical sciences in general, and practical social sciences in particular, as evidence against the legitimacy of the latter; rather, I would view it as a symptom of the inadequacy of the positivist standpoint in social sciences.

I even believe that the aforementioned practical sciences (in the sense of disciplines that teach us, based on our current insights, how certain human intentions can be most effectively realized under specific circumstances) will continue to exist and thrive in a time when the inadequacy of positivism will also be recognized in the field of theoretical social research.

The above objections against the legitimacy of independent practical economic sciences thus turn out to be misunderstandings overall. They are far from justifying the view that in the field of social research in general, and political economy in particular, the only alternatives to practical sciences are merely descriptions of what was and what is: "economic history and merely the description of past attempts to promote the economy and its developments."

History and statistics, in conjunction with common life experience, are important foundations for theoretical sciences, while these, in turn, serve as the basis for practical disciplines. The latter, therefore, also rely on experience—specifically comprehensive, critically validated, and systematically ordered experience. They are far from dismissing experience or underestimating its significance. History, morphology, and theory of economic phenomena are important, indeed indispensable auxiliary sciences for practical economic sciences, which have a fundamentally different task compared to the aforementioned disciplines.

As long as the practical surgeon and therapist do not restrict themselves solely to the study of anthropohistory, anatomy, and physiology, and the practical technologist does not limit themselves to the study of chemistry, mechanics, and physics, there will continue to be significant practical social sciences that are meaningful for practical life and the pursuit of knowledge, even at the risk that a misguided positivism may fail to incorporate these into its systematics of sciences.

If the practitioners of social sciences recognize that practical sciences pursue fundamentally different knowledge objectives than other economic sciences, then the current ambiguity regarding the pathways of knowledge and methods of practical sciences will also come to an end. By relying on historical and theoretical disciplines, practical sciences utilize experience to the greatest extent possible. However, in striving to establish the principles and methods for achieving human intentions, they do not limit themselves to merely presenting what the inventive human spirit has already practically validated in this respect. They do not confine themselves to previous experience; they are equally the result of combinatorial and inventive thinking, the genius of their practitioners. The progress in the field of practical sciences is not merely the result of accumulated knowledge but also of the inventiveness of those working in these fields.

The assumption that social sciences fundamentally have only to describe what was, what is, and how it has come to be, or what successes the efforts of acting individuals have achieved, would mean a renunciation of science in the face of any new societal needs for transformation, indeed a renunciation of any influence on administration in all those cases where there is no precedent so far. Not scientific research, but the administrative authorities, etc., will be the intellectual creators of every transformation in the field of practical economic sciences.

If it is now clear from the discussion that practical social sciences, alongside historical and theoretical social sciences, have independent significance and legitimacy—given that the knowledge objectives and methods of these sciences are different, and that their separate presentation is a requirement of the internal systematics of these sciences—then there can also be no doubt about the relationship between the morphology of social phenomena and practical social sciences. I have already pointed out that the morphological direction of research is justified in the field of economics.

Indeed, I do not hesitate to regard the fact that the methodological discussions of our historical economists have recently placed greater emphasis on the morphological perspective of research as a positive symptom of the emerging conviction within the historical school. This conviction acknowledges that our science must not only explore and describe concrete economic phenomena and their development—meaning our science is not merely a chronicle of events—but also address the generalities of economic phenomena.

In any case, those who would think that a morphology of economic phenomena could entirely replace practical economic sciences in general, and economic administrative science in particular, would fall into a new error. Even the theory of economics, which could closely relate to a morphology of economic phenomena in certain branches of the system (especially regarding the morphology of development), cannot in any way replace the latter.

Those who consider that only a morphology of economic phenomena and their development—alongside economic history and statistics—can be a legitimate branch of research in the field of economics overlook not only the independent task and significance of practical economic sciences but also that of national economic theory. They even go further than those who conflate economic theory with practical economic sciences, as they simultaneously confuse morphology and theory in the realm of national economic research.

## VIII: In defense against some recent attacks directed at my methodological standpoint

While I was busy writing this essay, I came across a lecture by L. Brentano titled "On the Causes of the Current Social Needs" and Fr. Kleinwächter's paper "Nature, Purpose, and System of National Economy." Both authors take the opportunity to present their methodological viewpoints, which stand in direct contrast to my own. Since their discussions have symptomatic significance for the prevailing views on the systematics of economic sciences, I would like to address them here.

Brentano adopts the scientific standpoint of the "laudator of Wakefield," arguing that the honest man who marries and raises a large family contributes greater benefits than the one who remains single and shirks responsibility. However, instead of drawing the obvious conclusion that the honest man who establishes or participates in cartels provides greater benefits than the one who merely discusses them, he arrives at the conclusion that endless talking about what and how things should be done, which comes into play to "do something," hinders the examination of the knowledge objectives and methods of research and leads to "intellectual indebtedness."

Now, I also believe that no matter how developed a methodology is, it is insufficient for the development of the sciences. There lies a tremendous gap between establishing methodology and achieving a satisfactory expansion of a science, a gap that can only be bridged by the genius of its practitioners. Positive research talent has often managed to achieve significant advancements in a field without a developed methodology, while methodology itself has never produced a science or transformed it in a groundbreaking manner without that talent. Methodology is of incomparable importance for secondary contributions in a science, but it is of far lesser significance for those major tasks whose resolution is reserved for genius.

However, as long as this genius has not yet emerged in our field, and as long as the development of important branches of political economy is hindered by misguided methodological doctrines, I believe we would do well not to underestimate methodological inquiries. As Kant stated, "It is already a great and necessary proof of intelligence or insight to know what one should reasonably ask." Why should investigations in the field of economics, which aim not only to instruct us on what one should reasonably ask but also to show how one arrives at reasonable answers to reasonable questions, be dismissed as "intellectual indebtedness"?

The natural sciences, in this regard enviable, have long since become aware of the system of their tasks and methods. Nevertheless, they do not shy away from methodological questions—especially not where serious doubts arise about the objectives and methods of research. If a group of natural scientists were to emerge that recognized only descriptive natural sciences, such as merely the morphology of natural phenomena or even just the theory of evolution as legitimate goals of research, while dismissing the exact natural sciences as mere play with concepts and viewing applied natural sciences as a misguided approach, then the methodological question would immediately come to the forefront of investigation in the field of natural sciences, provided that the unprejudiced sensibilities of the practitioners did not quietly overlook such one-sidedness.

In the field of social sciences, we are not in such a fortunate position. The nature of social phenomena and the impact that their distinct characteristics have on the objectives and methods of research are by no means clarified. Misunderstandings and prejudices have much greater scope here. Even one-sided views, like those mentioned above, are not outside the realm of possibility. Indeed, it is not inconceivable that prejudices of this kind could gain predominant acceptance in certain academic circles, leading individuals influenced by them to make decisions regarding the most important interests of our science. Who can assert that under such circumstances the methodological question is insignificant and is not, in fact, the most important and urgent issue we should all strive to clarify?

Oh, in our time, deeper transformations of the sciences—who would deny the need for such transformations regarding social sciences?—are still regarded as the result of naive, unreflected thinking. I will leave unaddressed whether even the critical reception of what others have researched is possible without methodological insights. However, it seems clear to me that the noblest blossoms of the German spirit have emerged from inquiries into "what should be done and how it should be done," and that this is in no small part how the character of German literary development has manifested itself. A respectable, though somewhat unclear scholarly effort regarding the objectives and methods of scientific research, I believe, has contributed to the rigidity of the historical school of German economists.

It is not as improbable as Brentano seems to suggest that a deepening into the methodological problems of our science will bring back to consciousness the system of tasks that economic sciences must address, thereby mitigating some of the detrimental one-sidedness in the development of economics in Germany. However, I maintain that through comprehensive methodological inquiries, not serving any immediate purpose, we can achieve an overview of the system of tasks that economic sciences must tackle. Occasional specialized investigations accompanied by methodological discussions—which, as is often the case, are the specific merit of those works—aim to illuminate the right aspects, but, by their very nature, carry the seed of one-sidedness within them.

The establishment of a methodology for the social sciences is the most important task of our time in the field of epistemology. The efforts of our most distinguished epistemologists are primarily directed towards the great goal of this "intellectual indebtedness." Truly, I would like to be that intellectual debtor who would resolve the methodological problem in the field of social sciences! Even the modest merit of having advanced its resolution by a significant step should, given the current state of methodological insights, still stand as high as the merit of any morphological monograph—such as those by Brentano regarding trade unions in England.

With his apparent disregard, Brentano speaks of the efforts of the "new abstract school" to subject national economic theory to the reform that this science so urgently needs to genuinely become a scientific foundation for practical economic sciences and thus for economic administration. He does not point out any errors by the "new abstract" theorists he criticizes in the realm of national economic theory; rather, he is insightful and sincere enough to acknowledge the progress that the latter owes to the group of scholars he opposes—progress that, curiously enough, has not come from the "historical-realist" school, which has existed for half a century, but from the supposedly life-averse "abstract school."

However, he never misses an opportunity to express his disdain for the "abstract theory," which he seems to regard as a mere play with concepts, because, well, it does not alleviate social needs. He finds the investigations of the "abstracts" worthless, even going so far as to describe the proponents of the "abstract school" as "incomprehensible," as their theoretical investigations do not avert "the social distress and the dangers to societal order that arise from it." I will deal extensively with this perspective elsewhere, particularly regarding the various directions of theoretical research and the exact national economy, and I will examine the issue of whether the accusation that "abstract" economics is merely a game with concepts—or, as some argue, a system of abstract propositions derived from certain aprioristic axioms—is justified.

These and similar prejudices, especially prevalent in the field of German national economics, will be the subject of my in-depth investigation. What I would like to note here regarding Brentano's arguments is that the standard of evaluation he applies to the theoretical efforts of the "abstracts" seems unyielding, regardless of which branch of economic theory is involved. Brentano overlooks that economic theory, even in the most realistically conceivable interpretation, must investigate the nature and relationships of economic phenomena and thereby achieve our understanding of them. The task of teaching us the principles and methods for purposeful intervention in the economy that correspond to the various conditions belongs, however, primarily to applied (so-called practical) economic sciences and, in particular, to economic policy. He overlooks the fact that no reproach can be directed at theoretical national economics or any specific branch of it for not addressing the problems that pertain to applied economic sciences.

How one-sidedly Brentano himself represents this standpoint can be illustrated by the fact that he deems the "abstract" theoretical national economics worthless, not because it fails to address the problems of economic welfare altogether. Instead, he dismisses all "examinations of concepts that fill the souls of the abstract theorists" precisely because the "abstract" theoretical national economics, which deals with a specific problem of welfare, is unable to eliminate "social dangers." This perspective recalls those well-known specialists in the field of medicine who may regard theoretical natural sciences as beautiful things, yet despise them for the reason that one cannot heal a diseased eye or a wounded leg with theories. Therefore, they cannot comprehend why anyone would spend time and effort—or even devote their entire life—to such theoretical investigations.

Brentano does not consider that he undermines his own morphological studies by claiming successes of this kind for the sciences. He is neither the intellectual creator of trade unions or conciliation offices nor, to my knowledge, has he directly brought such entities to life. He is not like Schulze-Delitzsch, who established those institutions but rather a commendable presenter and chronicler of them. Even if through these institutions, as Brentano believes or partly still assumes, social distress would be alleviated, even if he were to possess an impeccable foresight regarding their effects and developments, he could only claim the merit of a morphographer of those institutions, or of a national economic theorist regarding them.

It is not he, but the institutions he describes that would alleviate social distress, and likely even without his representations. However, no reasonable person would blame him for this, as he has contributed according to his abilities to what the morphology of specific types of economic phenomena should achieve. It would therefore be quite reasonable for him not to demand more from theorists than to provide what the theory, or specific branches of it, are inherently designed to deliver or to fulfill their respective tasks.

Brentano's insistence on the inadequacies of abstract economic theory appears more as an expression of frustration with the inability of theoretical frameworks to address pressing social issues. He fails to acknowledge that theoretical investigations can indeed complement practical efforts and provide the foundation for understanding the broader implications of economic phenomena. By dismissing theoretical contributions, he overlooks the potential for a productive dialogue between theory and practice, which is essential for addressing complex social problems.

In essence, the relationship between practical and theoretical disciplines in economics should be seen as synergistic rather than adversarial. Practical sciences provide the necessary tools and frameworks for implementation, while theoretical sciences offer insights and understanding that can guide effective interventions. Therefore, instead of pitting one against the other, it would be more beneficial to recognize the distinct but complementary roles that each plays in the pursuit of knowledge and the improvement of societal conditions.

While Brentano's criticisms of "abstract" economic theory are misguided, I believe there is a valid criticism I would like to raise against it: that in its current state, the tasks that an "abstract" theory of economics is meant to accomplish are only inadequately addressed.

Theoretical national economics would only fully fulfill its task if it not only provided us with the basic regularities in coexistence and succession, as well as empirical laws, but also elucidated the internal connections and understanding of economic phenomena. This, in turn, would establish the theoretical foundation for solving all problems of economic policy. The alleviation of social distress is not the only practical issue on which the science of economic welfare has proven its inadequacy due to previous deficiencies in theoretical understanding of the nature and relationships of economic phenomena.

The helplessness of administrative bodies in the face of economic crises, as well as the uncertain and tentative attempts of even the most distinguished state leaders regarding monetary, trade, industrial, and agricultural policies, are clear symptoms of the unsatisfactory state of practical national economics, which reflects the shortcomings of national economic theory itself.

The science of economic policy is, in its inadequacy, merely a correlative of a national economic theory that leaves the answers to questions—such as whether grain prices in countries with a predominance of grain imports affect grain prices, whether higher grain prices influence the price of bread, or whether taxes like coffee, petroleum, and other indirect taxes increase the prices of the related consumer goods—at the arbitrary discretion of politicians. No one is more acutely aware than we, who, as Brentano suggests, are filled with "abstractions," of the fundamental flaws of the prevailing national economic theory and its inadequacy as a foundation for applied economic sciences.

What distinguishes our perspective from Brentano's is the conviction that the science and practice of welfare can only be perfected through a deepening insight into the nature and internal relationships of economic phenomena. Just as in all other areas of practical activity, it is only through the progressive development of all branches of theory that the advancement of applied sciences and, consequently, the refinement of practice itself can occur. Therefore, it is among the most important tasks of those working in our field to cultivate the study of economic theory across all its branches. However, this task is hindered by misunderstandings and one-sided interpretations of its objectives, as well as by superficial remarks about the efforts aimed at reforming economic theory or its individual branches.

Brentano unfairly evaluates our theoretical investigations from the outset, suggesting that they should directly lead to the alleviation of social distress, which, as it seems to him, is an impossible demand. Yet, he also does not fully appreciate what they can already achieve according to their nature and tasks, or he presumes their truth without sufficient justification.

In conclusion, while there are certainly valid critiques of the current state of "abstract" economic theory, it is essential to recognize that the development of a robust methodology for social sciences is crucial. This methodology should not only aim to describe existing phenomena but also provide meaningful insights that can guide practical actions. Only by bridging the gap between theory and practice can we hope to address the pressing issues facing society today.

I would like to add one more remark here, which relates to Brentano's stance on practical economic sciences. I believe that Brentano engages in a rather excessive concern rooted in his inadequate understanding of the system of economic sciences when he asserts that theory should "master life."

False theories can indeed lead to significant issues and have often caused those practical sciences based on such theories to fall into their own errors. For example, misguided theories in anatomy and physiology have negatively impacted fields like surgery and therapy, influencing practical physicians in detrimental ways. Similarly, erroneous national economic theories have given rise to flawed economic policies. Misguided perspectives on the nature of national wealth and the function of money in the economy have contributed significantly to the persistence of erroneous mercantilist economic policies. Furthermore, the erroneous price theory of the classical school has profoundly influenced the practical demands of socialists, asserting that workers should receive the entire product or its price, thereby affecting the economy in substantial ways.

Indeed, false theoretical doctrines can undoubtedly be the cause of flawed practical theories and the misguided practices that stem from them. However, a theory that claims to "master life" is inherently contradictory. Economic theory can only present true or false laws regarding economic phenomena; it can analyze and interpret life, but it cannot master it, just as chemistry or physics cannot claim to do so.

Thus, when the question arises whether economic sciences have the task of "mastering" life, this inquiry can only pertain to practical economic disciplines. It is crucial to recognize the limitations of economic theory and its relationship to practice. The role of economic theory is to provide a framework for understanding and interpreting economic phenomena, not to dictate or control the complexities of real-life situations.

The essential task of economic theory is to uncover and articulate the laws that govern economic interactions and phenomena, allowing for informed decision-making in practical applications. However, the application of these theories in real-world contexts is contingent upon the specific circumstances and conditions of each situation. Therefore, while economic theory may inform and guide practical actions, it does not possess the power to master the multifaceted and dynamic nature of life itself.

In conclusion, we must be cautious of conflating theoretical insights with practical mastery. The value of economic theory lies in its ability to illuminate and explain economic realities, providing a basis for practical endeavors without overstepping its bounds. Only through a rigorous and reflective approach can we hope to navigate the complexities of economic life effectively.

If it is already recognized that the task of practical economic sciences is to teach us the principles and methods for the purposeful intervention of the state and subordinate organizations into the economy, then the above question must certainly be affirmed. The practical economic sciences inherently have the task of fulfilling this objective. They "master" the economy in much the same way that technology masters nature, and surgery and therapy master the human body. Therefore, practitioners of practical economic sciences can easily dismiss any criticisms leveled against them.

If there were a genuinely substantiated criticism, it could not imply that practical economic sciences do not have the task of shaping life at all, but rather that they are addressing this task in a misguided manner. Consequently, the question arises whether practical economic sciences should limit themselves to merely recording the results of past experiences or whether practitioners should be entirely prohibited, at least from the standpoint of strict scientific validity, from proposing means and methods for achieving human goals that are not drawn from previous experiences but instead result from combinatorial and inventive thinking.

In this regard, I believe that a science confined to merely describing existing institutions and administrative regulations and waiting for their results to "report" them would certainly lose any leading position in matters of welfare and would inevitably devolve into a mere historiography of the activities of administrative bodies and collectivist self-help institutions. No one would deny the significance of experience for practical sciences or even question it in the slightest. However, by demanding that practical disciplines be grounded in theoretical sciences, we are asserting that the former require the most comprehensive and critical empirical foundation, encompassing everything that can be "listened to from life."

Nevertheless, it would be to overlook the fact that numerous new arrangements in the economy depend on the practitioners of practical economic sciences. If these disciplines were merely recognized for the task of describing the past of relevant institutions and efforts and their successes, we would hinder progress. Brentano seems to overlook the great importance of combinatorial thinking and inventiveness for practical sciences and their application. If practitioners of practical disciplines and theorists were to share Brentano's view that science should focus solely on deciphering the developmental principles of life, and this became the exclusive rule of their actions, we would likely still be living in a world dictated by merely "listening to life," dressing in "life-gleaned" animal skins, and, without ideals stemming from principled values, still preserving serfdom and bondage.

Brentano has taken W. Roscher's statement, that our science has the exclusive task of "simply describing first the economic nature and needs of the peoples, secondly the laws and institutions that are established to satisfy them, and finally the greater or lesser success they have had," far too literally. This perspective on practical economic sciences and their tasks should, moreover—and this is perhaps its strongest aspect—not deter anyone from presenting new proposals for shaping economic life. If these proposals are correct and are implemented, it is likely that there will be those who will later "depict" the relevant transformations in practical life and once again "listen to" the principles underlying them.

However, what seems certain to me is that in the realm of practical economic disciplines, we can genuinely serve "science, the homeland, and humanity" not only through "descriptions" but also through combinatorial thinking and inventive spirit—especially when these are combined with rich experience. This approach can lead to meaningful contributions that advance both theory and practice, helping to address the pressing economic challenges of our time.

www.ingramcontent.com/pod-product-compliance
Lightning Source LLC
Chambersburg PA
CBHW070410230526
45471CB00006B/2745